T0380272

Beyond Imagination

DEVOTIONAL FOR THOSE
WITH MENTAL ILLNESS

JENNIFER STRIEGLE

WESTBOW
PRESS®
A DIVISION OF THOMAS NELSON
& ZONDERVAN

WestBow Press books may be ordered through booksellers or by contacting:

WestBow Press
A Division of Thomas Nelson & Zondervan
1663 Liberty Drive
Bloomington, IN 47403
www.westbowpress.com
844-714-3454

Because of the dynamic nature of the Internet, any web addresses or links contained in this book may have changed since publication and may no longer be valid. The views expressed in this work are solely those of the author and do not necessarily reflect the views of the publisher, and the publisher hereby disclaims any responsibility for them.

Any people depicted in stock imagery provided by Getty Images are models, and such images are being used for illustrative purposes only.
Certain stock imagery © Getty Images.

Interior Graphics/Art Credit: Jennifer Striegle

Unless otherwise indicated, scripture quotations are taken from the Holy Bible, New International Version®, NIV®. Copyright © 1973, 1978, 1984 by Biblica, Inc.™ Used by permission of Zondervan. All rights reserved worldwide.

Scripture quotations marked MSG or The Message are taken from The Message. Copyright 1993, 1994, 1995, 1996, 2000, 2001, 2002. Used by permission of NavPress Publishing Group.

ISBN: 979-8-3850-2175-8 (sc)
ISBN: 979-8-3850-2177-2 (hc)
ISBN: 979-8-3850-2176-5 (e)

Library of Congress Control Number: 2024905443

Print information available on the last page.

WestBow Press rev. date: 03/14/2024

To the man who always tucked me into bed after each terrible episode. When I say episode, I speak of a time when I got out of control due to my mental illness. The man is Craig, my second husband. He had to endure a huge amount of turmoil in our marriage. This book is only possible because he helped get me through the hard times.

I also want to give a mighty amount of credit to Althea, my therapist. She is the one who pushed me to write this book. Her wisdom was greatly appreciated.

Contents

Acknowledgments

All scripture is from the New International
Version unless otherwise stated.

Edited by Marjorie Emmert

Introduction

You Will Rejoice

Human bodies are puzzling, and mental illness plagues numerous people in the world today. "Mental illness impacts the lives of at least one in four adults and one in ten children—or sixty million Americans" (nami.org). I see a gap, though. Most churches don't truly address the issue of mental disease. It's not that they must address every health problem, but Christians seem to go the opposite way and say that belief in God can solve a person's mental problems, including actual disorders. I believe that the church needs to express the difference between worldly grief and hardship and the concrete health issue of mental illness.

People need to know it is OK to take medication, go to therapy, and work with medical doctors to treat their ailments, even their mental disorders. That doesn't mean that we should ignore the help of God. In Psalm 30:2 David called to God for help, and he healed him. We need to call to God also, and he will heal us. In Psalm 107:20 God "sent forth his word and healed them." Therefore, let us "give thanks to the Lord for his unfailing love and his wonderful deeds for men" (Ps 107:21).

Jesus told his disciples that their grief would turn to joy (Jn 16:22). One of the definitions of grief is "acute sorrow" or "intense emotional suffering." Sorrow isn't just ordinary but "acute"—meaning it's sharp. I know that in my life, I would describe my mental pain as "sharp." It is so comforting to know Jesus knows and understands. Jesus knew we would have deep sadness here on earth. How could we possibly escape it? We're not living in eternity yet with Jesus. As Christians, we long for the day we're with Jesus.

We "groan inwardly as we wait eagerly for our adoption as sons, the redemption of our bodies" (Rom 8:23). Sometimes when having trouble mentally, it's hard not to groan or want to groan. I know I feel like groaning and sometimes actually do. That gives us an idea of what Paul means in this verse. It also helps us understand our pain in general. We are not really at "home" yet with God. It is like we are homesick.

Grief will turn to joy, or great pleasure. That joy is equal and opposite of the grief. It is acute and intense. Just think. The joy will be as intense as the sorrow and pain. Jesus said to them, "You will rejoice." The time will come to truly rejoice forever. Hopefully, you can also come to rejoice here on earth. True rejoicing can only come from our father in heaven.

Jesus endured many hardships here on earth because he loved us beyond belief. He also said in John 16:33 that he told us these things so that in him "you may have peace. In this world you will have trouble. But take heart! I have overcome the world."

Jesus wants his children to make it through life with a heart for him. That is the reason I am alive today. I wouldn't be here if I didn't know God was here for me. I would have committed suicide. I know it is the weak way out, but I didn't care when the pain was so intense. It was a sharp mental pain that wouldn't let up even briefly, and even knowing it would get better eventually, I still couldn't bear it. I really don't know how I made it. The only answer is Jesus. Jesus loves you and does understand what you are going through. It's hard to comprehend, but only he truly knows your brain and heart.

I have been diagnosed with bipolar disorder and obsessive-compulsive disorder. I also have multiple sclerosis and narcolepsy. That doesn't necessarily mean I'll understand you if you have these, but it is to show you that I have a heart for those involved. My problem is unique to me, just as yours is unique to you. I have a bachelor's degree in biology with a minor in chemistry, so I am very interested in the physical and biological side of malfunctions of the body and brain. When it comes to nature versus nurture, I am mostly interested in the nature part at this point.

Many books have been written to help people deal with the nurture part as well as the situational side. This book is looking at mental disease from the perspective of it being a health issue. I want to give comfort and aid to those suffering with deep emotional pain caused by mental illness. I want to open the world as God sees it. Just like if someone had cancer and needed support, I want to give support for the chronic illnesses that can be categorized as mental disorders. They are chronic illnesses just like any other chronic illnesses.

At the end of every day's devotional, you'll find questions that will hopefully make you think. I recommend writing down the answers to solidify your thinking. Writing them down will put your thoughts and ideas into a concrete form requiring true contemplation of the questions.

Take this book and use it as you see fit. It is for you. My desire and prayer is that you may find hope and healing in these pages and the pages of the Bible. Whenever you have questions, go to the Bible. It really does have all the answers you need.

Day 1

DELICATE MACHINE

Our brains are works of art created by God. Illness transforms our bodies, including our brains. The brain is so complex that no one will ever discover everything about it. Diseases such as bipolar disorder and obsessive-compulsive disorder are difficult to understand. Each person's mental illness is unique; indeed, no two people have the same ailment. Treating the so-called "same affliction" will usually require different treatments.

Brains may contain similar mutations, but the rest of each person's brain is different. Also, a body is attached to the brain. Our bodies end up being exponentially varied. In other words, the differences between each person are endless. Not only are our brains different, but our other organs and bodily mechanisms are also different. It's no wonder that it is so hard to treat mental illness.

Jonathan Miller said, "Illness is not something a person *has*. It's another way of being." Being "sick" is just the way we are. That sounds negative, but that allows us to appreciate our unique being. It's a part of who we are. We can't just completely get rid of our adversity, like dropping off a package; it resides in us.

You can manage this inherent part of you. The word *inherent* means "existing in someone as a natural and inseparable quality," as *Webster's New World Dictionary* defines it. We can't separate ourselves from our mental illness, but we can learn to deal with it. Our brain is so complex and wonderfully made that only God can help us. It can be done because "all things are possible with God" (Mk 10:27).

Questions to Ponder

1. What do I know about my body? What is unique to me?

2. If your brain is a work of art, what does it look like? What kind of art is it?

Day 2
GREAT PHYSICIAN

In Psalm 30:1, David exalts God as one who lifts him "out of the depths," and God can do that for us also. Our distress at times is like "the depths." We feel so low and deep, but God can and will bring us "up from the grave" (Ps 30:3). Being on the brink of death when thinking of suicide is one way of looking at "the grave." He will spare you "from going down into the pit" (Ps 30:3) where there is no way out.

God knows everything, including how your brain functions. Since no two people have the same exact illness, only God can fully help. Family and friends will be able to help a little, but it takes an omniscient God to bring healing and reconciliation. Your body is a delicate machine that needs fine-tuning. God is the technician who will be doing that fine-tuning. Let him do that. He loves you very much and wants to fix the emotional engine he has created so intricately.

To supplement God's work, know yourself. After God, you know yourself the best. Trust yourself. I found that people will tell me different things, but deep down, I can tell what is indeed going on. Listen to your inner voice and pay attention. You are your best doctor here on earth. Be open and honest and speak up at doctors' appointments.

As the "great physician" and "wonderful counselor," God can and will use physicians and therapists to help you. Constantly pray that God will work through the doctors and therapists. He will do that. Even if the professionals aren't Christians, God is able to utilize them. He will be in them using their earthly bodies to do his will. Please never stop praying that God's will be done.

We are made in God's image. Our baseline of emotions and sensitivity is one that fits God's profile. It is in coming back to God and back to our origins that we truly find peace. As we begin to recover and head closer to what God wants us to be, we can remember that God is with us. He accepts us no matter what. He will always be everywhere—omnipresent—continually helping us.

Our bodies and brains are full of more good than bad since we are made in God's image. Remember that even though we feel full of much negativity, the good will win out. If our bodies were balances, the side with the good would be all the way down and the side with the bad would be all the way up because there are truly more positive things in our lives than negative.

The reason all of this is true is how God created us as human beings. He loved us so much that he made us in his image.

Prayer before an Appointment

Dear Father in heaven, you are the great physician and wonderful counselor. I praise you for who you are and what you do. I know you are here for me. You are omnipotent and omniscient. You know all things, including how my brain works because you made it. Sin came into the world and brought decay so that my brain isn't working correctly. You already know that, but I would like your will to be done today. Please come into my heart and brain and allow me to understand myself to the extent that I can help_____ (doctor or therapist) to help me. Please work through_____ (doctor or therapist). Give them the knowledge, understanding, compassion, and expertise to legitimately serve me. Work through _____. Allow them to see the truth and bring new light to my condition. Bring all the knowledge that they learned in school back to the forefront and help them to assimilate it into an answer for today. Work in their brain and heart to understand what I am saying. Allow your presence to be felt throughout this appointment. May the outcome be one that pleases you. Once again, let your will be done. It is in Jesus's name I pray. Amen.

Questions to Ponder

1. Who are my doctors and therapists that I need to keep in my prayers? How can I pray for them?

2. If your body is like a vehicle with an engine and everything, what kind of vehicle is it? What is wrong with it, and what can possibly be done to fix it?

3. What treatments are the doctors and therapists using to help me right now? What can I think of that can be done in addition to or instead of these treatments? Write down some of your ideas.

4. What are some things you can thank God for? What has he done for you so far? If you feel like he hasn't done anything, what would you like him to do? Ask God in prayer to do these things.

Day 3
FRUSTRATION

For the creation was subjected to frustration, not by its own
choice, but by the will of the one who subjected it, in hope that
the creation itself will be liberated from its bondage to decay and
brought into the glorious freedom of the children of God.
—Romans 8:20–21

We are in bondage to decay here on earth. Mental illness feels like decay. Decay implies a gradual, often natural, deterioration from a normal or sound condition, as *Webster's New World Dictionary* says. Our normal or sound condition would be what God originally intended us to be before the fall in the Garden of Eden. We were frustrated.

We are frustrated here on earth. The hope is that we will be brought into freedom—not just any freedom but glorious freedom. We are children of God and are loved by our Father in heaven. Take this into account and release your fears. The futility of our lives right now will be thwarted and changed to glory. God has the hope that we need. Our decaying bodies will be renewed.

This renewal is hard to grasp. Our brains are decaying presently. Our true freedom will come in heaven when our lowly bodies will be transformed "so that they will be like his glorious body" (Phil 3:21). In 1 Corinthians 15:35–58, Paul talks about the resurrection body and what it will be like: imperishable, glorious, powerful, and spiritual (vv. 42–43).

Paul also writes in this passage that God gives bodies, such as ours, as he has determined. He compares this growth to planting a seed to form a body. Every seed is unique, just like us. Even though we are all different, including our diseases, we need to work together to gain that freedom. This true freedom is from God. We will be free to be what God created us to be.

Humans, like plants, begin simply as seeds. All the genetic information for that living thing is contained in that seed. It grows into a unique creation, including any mutations. But the growth of the plant is subjected to weather and turmoil. We are also subjected to trouble in this world. Second Corinthians 4:8–9 says that "we are hard pressed on every side, but not crushed; perplexed, but not in despair; persecuted, but not abandoned; struck down, but not destroyed." Even though we are subjected to many things, God promises that we will survive. Hold on to that promise.

At first I couldn't understand despair because it seemed as though I had been in despair before. I looked up the word *despair* in the dictionary and found that I hadn't been in despair. It means to be without hope. Technically, I haven't been without hope. That hope is Jesus. It is always there, no matter what. Whenever you have trouble believing the Bible, do some research. The Bible is always true. There is probably some good explanation for what you are questioning.

Whenever you feel like you are in despair, say the Lord's Prayer. If you haven't memorized it, try to. It's hard to think straight sometimes. If you have a memorized prayer to repeat, it will be easier. Just say it repeatedly. If you're alone, you can say it out loud. If you're not alone, or you don't feel like saying it aloud, then think it in your head.

This doesn't mean anything unless you think about what you're saying. The memorization just gives you a foundation. The rest is in how you experience the prayer. The words are already there, but you must reflect on what the words mean.

The same is true if you read a prewritten prayer. Once again, you can read it aloud or to yourself and think about the words. One book that is very good about prayers is *Prayers That Avail Much* by Word Ministries. All the prayers are categorized and made up entirely of scripture.

Sometimes we don't even know what to pray for; therefore, embrace Romans 8:26. It reminds us that the Holy Spirit will help us. "We do not know what we ought to pray for, but the Spirit himself intercedes for us with groans that words cannot express." When you don't know what to pray, the Spirit helps you to pray. It may also be that you have an idea of what you want but don't know what you *ought* to pray. It may be different.

The Message translation of the Bible says that God's Spirit is "right alongside helping us along." How great is that! Also, it says that it doesn't matter if we don't know how or for what to pray. When you can't think straight, it is difficult to know how or for what to pray. This can give us comfort in knowing that God gives us a way out of our mess. He does the praying in us and for us.

Another thing about this verse, Romans 8:26, is the word *groans*. A part of my mental illness is groaning both out of mental pain and out of longing for God.

Groans do not contain words but are literally or mentally moans of distress, or as the Message says, "wordless sighs." It also says he is helping us by "making prayer out of our wordless sighs, our aching groans"

God knows us better than we know ourselves. He knows better what we need and want deep down inside. Let God infuse you with his Spirit and run away with your true groans. Romans 8 compares our pain to childbirth. God knows how deep our pain is and how much it hurts.

Questions to Ponder

1. How would you say you are "hard pressed on every side"? What feels like it is pressing in on you from all sides?

2. What perplexes you? What makes you uncertain, doubtful, or hesitant? What puzzles you or is hard to understand?

3. How do you feel persecuted? How are you afflicted or harassed? What constantly troubles or annoys you?

4. What has struck you down? Sometimes we feel like we're on the ground and can't get up. What has pushed you to that point?

5. Now think of ways that we are not crushed. What keeps us from truly being crushed to pieces?

6. Why aren't we in despair, based on the definition of despair? What is our hope?

7. Who keeps us from being abandoned? What keeps us from being forsaken or deserted?

8. How are we not destroyed? Why aren't we brought to total defeat?

Day 4

FEVER

One way to describe the spells or episodes that come over me is a "fever." It feels so good when it breaks. While it's happening, I feel "hot" and can't think. I also have this load I'm carrying that feels so heavy that I almost can't carry it. The stress and anxiety levels go up, and I can't seem to breathe freely. Once the "fever" has broken, it's like I have put down my load and suddenly feel cooler. A peace comes over me, and I can think again. My world begins to expand, and things seem possible. I can concentrate on doing God's will and trying to gain health.

If this is the way you feel sometimes, then be happy when the relief comes, and try to remember how it feels. The next time you develop that "fever" you can have hope that restoration will come. You may have chills at the beginning. Anxiety sometimes causes you to literally shake, like when you are cold. The heat begins to build up and cause mental confusion. Once the fever breaks, you sweat. Just like your body releasing water, your spirit releases all the negative emotions. What's left is a clear mind full of anticipation.

"Be joyful in hope, patient in affliction, faithful in prayer" (Rom

12:12). Therefore, joy comes from hope. No matter what comes your way, you can know that God will get you through. When you are having an episode, take a deep breath, put a cold rag on your head, and run cold water over your wrists. Trust that God will get you through it. Look to heaven for your hope despite the awful feelings. Then deep down you will have joy because hope arises. You may not be happy, but joy and hope are different than happiness. Strive to be patient throughout your worst times. Never stop praying that God will release you from your bondage.

When you have that "mental fever," you may need to go to the doctor; therefore, go to someone for help. Someone else may be able to assist you in getting rid of your fever. Just like medicine, they may be able to give you coping skills to treat the sickness. When you can't think for yourself, they can think for you.

Questions to Ponder

1. What do you feel like when you have a fever?

2. What do you do to rid yourself of the fever?

3. How can you relate a physical fever to a mental fever?

4. What does it feel like to have joy or hope?

5. Who can you go to for assistance to heal yourself? What can they do to help?

Day 5

YOU'RE OK!

You are OK! No matter what anyone tells you, you are normal and all right. Even though you may be different than other people, you are made the way God intended. Everyone is different in one way or another. You're just different in a way that is hard for people to understand. That doesn't make it bad or negative. Please understand that God loves you and wants the very best for you.

Other people are another story. We are in quite the predicament with those people who don't understand mental illness. I am disappointed in society. I work in a pharmacy and observe misinterpretations quite often. Someone who works in the pharmacy, like a pharmacist or pharmacy technician, knows what medications someone is taking and makes a comment about what that person is like. We don't know a single thing about that person's mental state; therefore, it would behoove us to give them the benefit of the doubt.

When a person is known to be taking a certain medication, it doesn't warrant a judgment of any sort. Unfortunately, it seems like a judgment is often made. Whether intentional or not; usually the judgment is negative in some way. Giving a person the benefit of the doubt is often not what is done. For instance, if a person is taking a medication for his or her heart, it doesn't necessarily mean that the person is not taking care of his or her body. There are other possibilities as to why a person is taking a medication.

Mental illness is the same way. Many possibilities arise as to why a person is taking a certain medication. Also, even if you knew exactly why a person is taking a medication, you do not know what's going on inside his or her head. The ramifications of the disease or medicine may not all be apparent. That is why no judgment should be made about a person. No presumptions should be made.

With all, don't make presumptions about yourself either. We need to remember that God made us special and good. He knows us inside and out. He doesn't judge us, so neither should we judge ourselves. Always give yourself the benefit of the doubt. Even though we may not even understand our own bodies and minds, God does and still loves us.

Questions to Ponder

1. What are some presumptions that people have made about you over the years? How did you feel?

2. How have you judged yourself and condemned yourself for things that have happened?

3. How has God made you mentally special?

Day 6

GOOD GIFTS

All good gifts are from God, so cherish every good thing in your life no matter how small. "Every good and perfect gift is from above, coming down from the Father of the heavenly lights, who does not change like shifting shadows" (Jas 1:17). Try to be content with the small as well as the big gifts. Something as small as getting to work without an accident or as big as winning the lottery should both generate praise.

Looking over your life, you may see both good and bad things. We try to hold onto the good things, and then, also unintentionally, we hold on to the bad. We, therefore, have a lot of baggage—both good and bad. We need to proceed forward without holding onto these things in the wrong way. Dwelling on past positive events too much will lead to depression if we can't seem to achieve that event again. Also, if we think about what has happened in the past in a negative way, we lose hope.

Drop off that baggage, and look to the future. Hope and grasp onto the positive so that wonderful things can happen. By "great" things, I don't mean something huge but anything that glorifies God.

We need to cherish the past but move toward the future. Also, if you have had trouble in the past with an aspect of your mental illness, it doesn't mean it will happen again. Two things may come into play: your brain may have changed, or you have learned new techniques to fight this enemy.

Remember that you are "fearfully and wonderfully made" (Ps 139:14). God made us in such a way as to warrant awe and reverence. We have no way of fully comprehending how we are made, but knowing that God knows is comforting. Not only did God create us, but he created us infinitely complex and amazing. Considering yourself down to the core of your cells and DNA, you can appreciate God's work.

Psalm 139 also says God "created my inmost being" (v. 13). That means that God manufactured our deepest emotions and soul—including our mental capacity and sense of self. Our awareness of this has the potential to initiate praise—praise to God for his unfailing love, despite all odds. The center, or nucleus, of our being is one approved by God. Only God can fathom your existence and who you truly are. Let him be your soul mate, and talk to him often.

You are important, "for it is God who works in you to will and to act according to his good purpose" (Phil 2:13). Even though God knows you perfectly, all your thoughts and actions, he still wants to use you. He has a purpose for you and will perform his acts of righteousness through you. God works through you to accomplish his purpose and miracles—even in the lives of others. He sees through the negative to bring about the positive.

Ephesians 2:10 states that "we are God's workmanship, created in Christ Jesus to do good works, which God prepared in advance for us to do." God's handiwork is a polished piece of art—you. God crafted us with skill and technique to do that for which he has already prepared. God has everything laid out for you. Many good deeds have been set in place especially for you. These are things that only you can do.

Questions to Ponder

1. What are some ways you see that you are "fearfully and wonderfully made"? Think about your body and the science that comes into play.

2. What are some good gifts that God has given you? They can be as little or as big as you want.

3. Name some ways God is using you right now and some ways he could use you in the future.

4. What are some unique characteristics for which God can design special works? How are you different from other people, and what makes you special? What unique events have occurred in your life to make you who you are?

5. What are a few physical characteristics that make you unique? (This will also help you to see the creative art that you are. God is not boring. No other person in the entire world is like you mentally or physically.)

6. What baggage are you holding onto? (Both good and bad ...)

Day 7

WHY REJOICE?

Anxiety is a demon that rips through the lives of many people, but some people experience it more intensely. Some people have life events that they must tackle, while others bear this burden for no apparent reason. Both are equally hazardous. Both are penetrating and deep. It affects not only our minds and thoughts but also our physical bodies. In a panic attack the heart beats rapidly, and hyperventilation may occur. Both can be terrifying. You feel claustrophobic and unable to proceed.

So, why rejoice? The answer lies in the Bible. Philippians chapter 4 gives us a command to rejoice. If you want to please God, follow his commands. Immediately following, Paul says not to be anxious about anything. To me that means that rejoicing and anxiety are opposite forces. Also, in that same paragraph it explains that peace will come. This equation, relating rejoicing to worrying, equals peace in the end. Rejoicing minus worry equals zero, and peace is what everyone wants.

But what is rejoicing, really? It's celebrating God in a jubilant way with much joy and thanksgiving. It's reveling in who God is and what he has done. When it seems nothing is enjoyable, just enjoy God, and instead of worrying, pray. Prayer is what you add to rejoicing to counteract fretting; it's all part of the equation of peace.

Rejoice + Prayer − worry = Peace

"Let petitions and praises shape your worries into prayers, letting God know your concerns" as the *Message* version of the Bible says in Philippians 4:6. Imagine how strong the prayers would be, considering how strong the worry is! If the same power of the anxiety is harnessed into prayer, then the prayers would be intense. The more intense the prayer, the closer to God you would be. So, flip your anxiety around, and use that intensity to pray even more deeply.

Questions to Ponder

1. How has anxiety changed your life?

2. What are some physical changes that have occurred due to anxiety? What are some emotional changes that anxiety has caused?

3. Even though it may be difficult, what are some ways you can rejoice in the Lord?

Day 8

THE PEACE OF GOD

The peace of God transcends all understanding. Peace is the main thing that one needs when anxiety hits, and anxiety is the one thing that infiltrates all the other mental disorders. Despite what you do, anxiety still prevails sometimes. But God knows this and does give us a way out!

Philippians 4:4–9 describes a journey to peace—starting with rejoicing. The paragraph starts the journey at rejoicing and ends in peace. It continues about peace in the second paragraph as well. At the very end of that section—the very end of our journey—Paul says, "And the God of peace will be with you." Between rejoicing and having peace is the main part of the trip.

The very first thing that Paul says is, "Rejoice in the Lord always." He doesn't say rejoice at just certain times but *always*. What a difficult concept to grasp! But what exactly does *rejoice* mean? It has to do with delight in the Lord. The part that is interesting is that the prefix *re* can mean" back" or "returning to a previous state." So that infers that we are going back to a state of joy and delight.

It should also be anew each time we rejoice and express joy in the Lord again and again.

The word *always* hands us the task of rejoicing even in suffering. Christ has done so much for us that we have great reason to rejoice and have joy. It is important to fix our thoughts on Jesus so that we can feel his presence.

Strangely enough, the next sentence reveals a unique step toward peace—gentleness. This gentleness that is supposed to be evident to all is a key to combatting anxiety. An aspect of this gentleness is gentleness with you. You need to be gentle when confronting yourself because we are delicate and breakable. Just like dealing with a crystal glass, we must hold onto ourselves firmly so as not to be dropped, yet without roughness or harshness. This may even mean talking to yourself like you would to a baby or child.

Next comes the antidote to worry—thanksgiving, along with prayer and petition. As the NIV commentary states, "Anxiety and prayer are two great opposing forces in Christian experience." God is there; run to him in prayer! It is here that peace finally comes. We can't comprehend God's peace, so just bask in it.

Safety is sometimes a concern on a journey, so consider the next statement. The peace of God will guard your hearts and your minds in Christ Jesus. The NIV commentary says this is a military concept depicting a sentry standing guard. God is strong and can firmly guard every part of your being.

The commentary goes on to say that God's "protective custody" of those who are in Christ Jesus extends to the core of their beings and to their deepest intentions.

Questions to Ponder

1. How can you be gentler to yourself? List ways you can show gentleness to yourself.

2. How has God kept you safe during your times of mental confusion?

Day 9

FEAR

Anxiety is fear, but we don't have to be afraid of anything when God is with us. Try to rely solely on God and his strength. Hopefully, that will begin to penetrate our souls and help our physical manifestations of anxiety. God made our bodies very specific in how they react to fear. He made it to protect us, but sometimes it gets out of whack and causes us to react in a way disproportionate to our situation.

The sympathetic division of the autonomic nervous system plays a crucial role in the way our bodies react to anxiety. This system is also known as the fight-or-flight system. Whether it is legitimate fear of a threatening situation or an unknown feeling of doom, our bodies react the same way. Our heart starts pounding and our breathing becomes deeper and more rapid. We may get cold, sweaty skin, and our pupils may dilate. God created all these bodily functions. God uses these functions to bring our bodies back to homeostasis.

Mental illness and anxiety take our bodies out of homeostasis, so God has to almost mechanically bring us back into balance. Take hold of your anxiety and embrace it as a transition to peace. Once this battle is over and the storm passes, peace comes. God also made the parasympathetic system to bring us back to rest. Remember that our bodies are miraculous and can take care of us.

In the concluding section of Paul's journey to peace (Phil 4:8–9) he exhorts us to think about certain things. In the *Message* version of the Bible these things are listed as "true, noble, reputable, authentic, compelling, gracious, the best, the beautiful, and things to praise. Our minds should be focused on these positive characteristics, not negative. It's hard, but that's part of our recovery. The more we think about such things, the more our mind transforms into a place of complete rest.

Later in chapter 4 of Philippians, Paul speaks personally to the Philippian church who "went alongside him in his troubles," as it says. It's good for us to find fellow Christians who can stand beside us and help us. The prayers of others will strengthen our requests to God. And don't forget to thank them like Paul did!

God does not leave us alone to fight our battles. At the end of our journey to peace we find out that God who is the God of peace is with us. He will show us how to deal with worry and anxiety and then give us the strength and knowledge we need. He will not leave us alone, and he will not judge us when we have trouble relaxing.

Questions to Ponder

1. What is "true" in your life? Is there someone who is faithful, loyal, and/or constant? What is certain or accurate? Is there something reliable in your life? Genuine?

2. Can you think of something that is "noble" or someone who is "noble"? Special? Exalted?

3. What or who is "reputable"? What is respectable or decent?

4. Think about something that is authentic. List those items or people. Are they genuine and trustworthy?

5. *Compelling* is an interesting word to contemplate. What is compelling? Irresistible?

6. Name something "gracious"—gentle, kind, charming.

7. Finally, write down things that are beautiful and right. Think of the best things in your life.

Don't forget to dwell on places that you have been and interesting people you've met in your life. Build up your repertoire of thoughts by writing them down and thinking of your whole life, not just the present. Take yourself to a time or place that gave you comfort or solace.

Day 10

THE LORD WHO COUNSELS ME

Medication is important in recovery from explicit mental disasters, but counseling and therapy need to be a part of any rehabilitation. The implicit qualities of mental illness need to be addressed. Some things are not plainly expressed or apparent to the patient. A therapist/counselor can sometimes help. The greatest counselor, of course, is God. In Psalm 16:7, David says the Lord counsels him. He can counsel us in the same way. God can not only counsel in his own way using scripture and internal thoughts from the Holy Spirit in us but can also work through people here on earth.

In writing this book, I went through a period of severe depression and didn't write at all. I kept crying out to God to help me. I didn't have any hope of getting better, and I wanted to die. I felt disappointed in myself that I wasn't using everything about which I was writing. The reason I'm telling you this is that I understand and want to help. There is hope. I now am on medication that is helping me.

Two things are important in this situation. God decided to help me using medication, but it took a while. He can primarily use medication, and it's OK. I still think counseling is important, but it won't get anywhere until your medication is stable. The second point is that even though I doubted God, he stayed near to me and didn't leave me. He'll never leave you.

David gives us comfort at the end of Psalm 16 when he expresses the gifts of joy and pleasures given to us. Basically, it is about heaven, but any mention of joy and eternal pleasures can be comforting. God will fill you with joy in his presence, with "eternal pleasures" at his right hand (verse 11).

Isaiah expresses God in 28:29 as "wonderful in counsel and magnificent in wisdom." God is the best counselor. Wonderful means his counsel/advice is amazing and marvelous. We get this counsel through the Bible and the Holy Spirit inside us. His wisdom is awe-inspiring with vast knowledge and understanding. He knows everything; not only knows it but understands it.

David once again mentions counseling in Psalm 142:1–2 by telling us that he "cried aloud to the Lord" and he "lifted his voice to the Lord for mercy." Then he "poured out his complaint before God" and "told him his trouble." Counselors help us in this way. We not only need to pour out our hearts to a human counselor but also, more importantly, to God. He can help us.

"Wait for the Lord; be strong and take heart and wait for the Lord" (Ps 27:14). Waiting is oppressive, but we must be patient. "But if we hope for what we do not yet have, we wait for it patiently" (Rom 8:25).

We may "groan inwardly" as we wait, as it says in Romans 8:23. Groaning is a common product of intense pain—physically or mentally. That means waiting is not easy. Keep on going with the assistance of counselors, including God.

Imagine waiting in a line at an amusement park. It's annoying and frustrating, but at the end of the line is an exciting attraction.

If you wait on the Lord, heaven is at the end of the journey. Also, imagine sitting in a waiting room at the doctor's office. You may read a magazine or book while you wait. In life, you do and achieve many different things along the way in the same way. While waiting, remember to read the Bible and pray as you head toward the finish line.

Questions to Ponder

1. What would you ask God if you were standing with him face-to-face?

2. What do you like in a counselor? How is God like that?

3. How have you doubted God in the past, or how are you doubting him now? Then write how you desire for God to help you. What would you like God to do?

4. What's it like waiting on God?

   Isaiah 28:29; 9:6

   Psalm 16:7

Day 11

TAKE HEART

Take heart! Even though our lives are fraught with profuse pain, we can still work at making our lives better. Singing, playing a musical instrument, drawing, and many other things can give us new life. Once we reach higher ground and are no longer drowning in a sea of emotion, we can commence to concentrate on other details. These details can then multiply our happiness and peace. It is tough to do anything additional while feeling out-of-sorts. You will probably have to wait until some healing arrives.

Carbon Leaf, a musical group, has a song that describes this: "Once the tears have dried life goes on." You must take care of the physical/biological aspects of your illness before you can deal with therapy and circumstances.

After you experience a moment of health and healing, begin to look to the future and what you can do to multiply your happiness. Your brain can actually change physically when subjected to new endeavors. This physical alteration will make it easier next time you have trouble. There is a physical change that comes about in those with obsessive-compulsive disorder. Whenever I get "stuck" in a ritual or counting, I have to stop myself. It is almost impossible to do, but once I do it, it will be a little easier next time to stop. My doctors and therapists confirmed that there is evidence that an actual physical change occurs in the brain every time I stop. Recognizing this may lead to an improvement with OCD (obsessive-compulsive disorder).

It may be that something similar happens in our brains any time we do something good and positive for our bodies and brains. For instance, if we stop crying when we need to cry, maybe next time it will be less difficult to stop. Especially in this case, you might have to be on the correct medication first before you can stop at all. There have been many times that I literally couldn't cease to cry. When I got on a better medication, I might still cry, but at least I could stop eventually.

On a more positive note, if you start doing something that brings some confidence or enjoyment, maybe a chemical change happens in your brain. The chemical change will enable you to do more next time and so on. That chemical change will not only enable you to do more but also to do something in a more enjoyable way each time. Once again, everything then multiplies itself, and you do better.

Questions to Ponder

1. What have I done in the past that caused me immense joy? If you can't think of anything, what do you wish would cause you to have great joy?

2. What have you done in the past that was creative or unique? Has there been anything you've done that you can't believe you did? For example, I once drew a pencil drawing of my grandma

that was good. Today I can't believe I really did it. It seems impossible now.

3. What is something that you think you could do or want to do that you haven't done yet? Maybe it's playing a musical instrument or painting a picture. Or, maybe it is as simple as putting together a puzzle or making a craft. Just write something down that interests you or you think would interest you.

4. What are some daily things you could do to add life to your days? For instance, would you play a board game? Would you play a video or computer game? Would you write a short poem?

Day 12
THANKS

A preacher's wife once told me that she thanks God as many times as she asked for something. In other words, if I asked for God to help me over and over, I then thank him over and over. I genuinely experience a release and love God even more. God wants us to thank and praise him. We should be willing to spend time with God in prayer, not only asking for things, but telling him how wonderful he is.

As far as thanking goes, it is also a neat idea to thank God for little things as you go along in life. For instance, when I go to fill up my cup with a soft drink at work, I thank God that it's not flat. There have been times in the past when the fizz was gone, and my drink was flat. So, whenever I go to fill up and it's good, then I thank God. God likes us to thank him for everything. Also, it's good to thank God for things he will do in the future. It shows him that you trust that he'll do them.

Another thing you can do when you get in a jam is try to sing— something simple and easy. If it is too complicated, it will be harder to do. Pick a basic church song, like a children's song that you sang when you were little. Another good option would be a hymn because hymns are not only straight-forward but also have a lot of meaning and emotion. Sing it aloud or hum it when you are alone at home or in your car. Try singing it in diverse ways to see which way brings you the most comfort at the time. It may be different on various occasions. Try it faster or slower, or louder or softer.

When trying to get through a day, you can also repeat positive truths over and over to yourself, either aloud or in your head. Think of a short phrase, a short Bible verse, or a positive word. Just say it to yourself, emphasizing each word one at a time because that will give new meaning to the statement each time. A truth is better than a command so choose wisely. Using the word *smile* is more of a command and may put pressure on yourself, but if you say, "I am smart" or "I can do all things through Christ who strengthens me" (Phil 4:13), then you may feel empowered.

When thinking of things to say to yourself, be positive yet realistic. Maybe you could sit down and write out some things, especially good things about yourself and good things you can do. Be creative and ask for help from a close friend or family member. Remember, say things that make you feel good about yourself and good in general.

Questions to Ponder

1. What are some things you could do that would directly benefit your brain or body? These might be such things as exercise or memorizing scripture.

2. Name a few songs you know and could sing. Write out the words if you want.

3. Write out the Lord's Prayer and/or another prayer you have memorized or want to memorize.

Try to imagine yourself doing some of these things. Picture yourself doing one or two of them. The next step will be to literally do one or two of them, but don't think of too much at once, or you won't do them or be able to do them. Also, please remember that you don't have to be perfect or even close to perfect. God is already happy with you. He doesn't care if things are or aren't perfect. He loves you no matter what.

The point is to explore and try new things, like exercise or memorizing scripture; that will not only directly help you but also will glorify God. Drawing a picture or singing a song can obviously glorify God, as well as anything for which you give thanks and praise to God. Not only will these things directly help you, but also once you do them it will multiply your confidence, creativity, and motivation. Because of that, you may be able to do even more, and the multiplication will never end.

Day 13
GROANING

You may be wearied by the burdensome thought of going up a flight of steps to obtain knowledge and relationship with God. You may have been told, or just thought, that even salvation is a step-by-step process. I'm here to tell you, with the help of Oswald Chambers (as told from *My Utmost for His Highest*, p. 210), that "we are either there, or we are not."

That may sound intimidating at first, but, once you soak it in, you realize it truly isn't. Obedience—pure and simple obedience—opens all his great revelations and allows you to know God. It is as simple as that. Obey what you know already, then God will reveal more truth about himself. Don't worry, therefore, about "finding out" God's plan. Just obey, and he will show you the way.

Chambers believes the "conception of practical work that has not come from the New Testament, but from the systems of the world in which endless energy and activities are insisted upon, but no private life with God" is "the great enemy to the Lord Jesus Christ."

As you are contemplating things today, relax and realize that your energy can be saved for only the most important of endeavors.

Reaching and pleasing God is not one of those. He will be running to you if you are willing to reach out your hand to him.

Cling to God as David does in Psalm 63:8. Also, "cling to what is good" (Rom 12:9). Your joy may be complete then. "Ask and you will receive, and your joy will be complete." (Jn 16:24). Joy propels us to leave depression and proceed to happiness in the Lord. Sometimes our joy seems incomplete, but it can be complete with Christ. "The Lord is good, a refuge in times of trouble. He cares for those who trust in him," (Na 1:7). "Cast all your anxiety on him because he cares for you." (1 Pt 5:7). Therefore, ask and trust. You can give all, not just part, of your anxiety to God. He is there and listens. When you feel anxious or depressed, throw those feelings far away to God.

A major part of mental illness is a fair amount of groaning. The Bible speaks of groans many times. "We know that the whole creation has been groaning as in the pains of childbirth right up to the present time. Not only so, but we ourselves, who have the first fruits of the Spirit, groan inwardly as we wait eagerly for our adoption to sonship, the redemption of our bodies" (Rom 8:22–23).

Within our waiting come groans because we must wait patiently for God's final adoption of us. We are already children of God, but the final inheritance comes later in heaven. Also, sometimes it is hard to know what to pray for. "In the same way, the Spirit helps us in our weakness. We do not know what we ought to pray for, but the Spirit himself intercedes for us through wordless groans" (Rom 8:26). The Holy Spirit truly helps us when we have nothing left but groans. Our minds may become jumbled, but God pulls us through.

Questions to Ponder

1. What have you been trying to accomplish by actions and just trying really hard rather than just letting go?

2. What are things your energy should be used to accomplish instead of pleasing God?

3. How has God shown his great love for us? Why can we know that we can trust him to take care of us even if we are leaving the steps up to him? How does grace and mercy play a part in all this?

Day 14

CHOICES

Nature has a way of drawing us closer to God, but it also has a way of leading us to both enthusiasm and peace. Our wild and vivid imaginations allow us to come near to our vulnerable selves. If we are exposed, then we can truly see what's around us—the vastness, the beauty, and the fragile world.

If you are blowing up a balloon, your breath might represent the many ideas that you have about yourself. The balloon is what you become based on your thoughts. If someone comes along with a pin, they may poke a hole in the balloon and burst the balloon. That would represent a slight cut of disapproval. At this point it is up to you to be passionate about yourself and treasure whatever the balloon used to be—the color, the design, etc.

The following is a list of choices that you could make in life, relative to your mental health. Think about these things and then write down your choices when you get a chance:

- medicines you take
- physicians you see

- kinds of physicians you see
- category of drugs you use
- therapists you see
- if you see a doctor
- if you see a therapist
- if you take medicine
- if you listen to your doctor
- if you listen to your therapist
- if you go to more than one doctor or therapist
- if you get a second opinion
- if you take your medicine as you should
- if you self-medicate

Doctors can also make choices:

- which medicines to recommend
- prescribe just one medication or more and in what combination

God gives us choices. Don't give up on yourself or your doctor or God. God will keep working through you and your doctor and your therapist if you let him. This will especially be true if you ask. Relax and let go and let God. God answers prayer: God will not give up on you no matter what.

God will bring people into your life at various times in your treatment, recovery, disease, and peaceful times as well who will encourage you. As the saying goes, "Coincidence is when God works a miracle and decides to remain anonymous." Jesus also promises us the Holy Spirit—"an advocate to help you and be with you forever" (Jn 14:16). This advocate will be a teacher, reminder, and counselor. "But the Advocate, the Holy Spirit, whom the Father will send in my name, will teach you all things and will remind you of everything

I have said to you" (Jn 14:26). An advocate acts on your behalf as a counselor who helps and comforts. "But when he, the Spirit of truth, comes, he will guide you into all the truth" (Jn 16:13). He is our source of truth in this world. He is our guide, speaker, and informer of truth.

Questions to Ponder

1. Go over the list of choices and write out some of your choices.

2. What are some things people say or do showing disapproval to burst your bubble?

3. How does nature point you toward God?

4. What are some ways that you see the Holy Spirit as:

   Counselor—

   Guide—

   Comforter—

   Helper—

   Advocate—

   Teacher—

   Reminder—

   Speaker and informer of truth—

   Encourager—

Day 15
ABANDON

Live in complete abandon. Abandon that life, not just of sin but of depression and mental illness. Lose it, leave it behind, forget it, lay it down, shake it off, wash it off. If it is too hard, then keep asking for God's help. Listen to the voice of truth, not the lies of the devil. The outside may seem flimsy or in-the-works, but deep down God has laid the foundation in you.

Hope can change everything. It lifts us up with every dream and every step. It starts down low, though—on our knees. We are strongest on our knees in prayer. Strengthen your knees. Scar your knees even. God will heal them. Let the scars be reminders of earnest prayers sent up to heaven constantly and persistently. Then grab onto that peace God will impart to you.

Because of God's great compassion, he does not abandon us (Neh 9:19). "The Lord is compassionate and gracious, slow to anger, abounding in love" (Ps 103:8). Even in your worst times, God will not leave you.

Paul and Timothy experienced many trials and tribulations in the province of Asia as it says in 2 Corinthians 1:8. Paul says they were "under great pressure, far beyond [their] ability to endure." He says they "despaired of life itself." Does that sound familiar? In today's world, pressure persists day by day. Many people contemplate suicide. They want a way out. Mental illness may only accentuate that feeling. This doesn't have to be a sentence of death," as the Bible calls it. Paul clarifies it by explaining that "this happened that we might not rely on ourselves but on God (v. 9).

When the problems come, release them to God. Rely on God. Let God carry you through. He will hold onto you and help you endure any troubles. We may not have the ability to endure them, but God does.

"Whatever is true, whatever is noble, whatever is right, whatever is pure, whatever is lovely, whatever is admirable—if anything is excellent or praiseworthy—think about such things" (Phil 4:8). "And the God of peace will be with you" (Phil 4:9b). Put your thoughts in God's hands, and you shall receive peace. This peace will sustain you through your darkest times.

Remember that "our citizenship is in heaven. And we eagerly await a Savior from there, the Lord Jesus Christ, who, by the power that enables him to bring everything under his control, will transform our lowly bodies so that they will be like his glorious body" (Phil 3:20–21). We are waiting, but the result is fantastic.

Questions to Ponder

1. When can you make time to get down on your knees and pray? How long will you allow to pray? What types of things will you pray?

2. Who has abandoned you in life? What did it feel like?

3. What pressure do you feel today? What trials and tribulations are you enduring?

4. How has God shown you compassion?

Day 16

MAP IT!

Our lives are like maps with all the various land features. Plus, everyone has varying types of formations within his/her own publication. Just like each state in the United States may have its own individual map, each person has his or her own. These maps reveal truths about each human and how his or her brain works. The specific details on the display of the land/life open a world of possibilities.

For instance, a person who is in depression represents certain formations. The map shows a ravine that runs the length of the page from west to east. The roads around it have been traveled well. A river runs nearby that represents the times in this person's life when life runs more smoothly. A few hills are present, which show the presence of the highs in life. Some of the roads are roundabouts so that the traveler goes around in circles sometimes in life. Some of the roads are straight, and some of the roads are curvy.

Through all this, God is the cartographer and creator. He is the person who made all the formations and designed all the intricate details of our world. He also put the details in place in our heads. He knows how to help us in our time of need. He *is* the guide who can get us to any location safely and soundly. He knows the way; he is the way. Trust in him, and he will lead you home. Jesus said, "I am the way and the truth and the life" (Jn 14:6). Right before that, John says "Do not let your hearts to be troubled (Jn 14:1).

In the Bible, Joseph had a diverse map of a life. His story is recorded in Genesis chapters 37–48. At seventeen his brothers hated him because his father loved him more than them. They were going to kill him but decided to sell him instead. It all worked out for good in the end, but there were bumps along the way. Joseph could have given up, but he didn't.

Joseph was put in charge of Potiphar's household until he was falsely accused of betraying him. He was then imprisoned for several years. While in prison, he interpreted dreams and gained respect. Later, this got him released, and the Pharaoh put him in charge of the land. When it came time for the dreams to be fulfilled, there came seven years of abundance and then seven years of famine. During the famine, Joseph's family came to Egypt for aid. That's where they saw Joseph again and reunited. In the end he was there to save his family. Joseph even says to his brothers, "Do not be angry with yourselves for selling me here, because it was to save lives that God sent me ahead of you" (Gn 45:5).

Even though Joseph knew the good that came from everything, he also knew pain. One can see that through the names of his children. His firstborn was named Manasseh because God made him "forget all [his] trouble" (Gn 41:51). His second was named Ephraim because "God has made me fruitful in the land of my suffering" (Gn 41:52). We may also have trouble and suffering, but God can help us continue past all of that.

Questions to Ponder

1. What are some different spots on a map that you can think of, and what do you think they represent?

2. What details are on your map?

3. How is God helping you?

Day 17

FAITH

You are strong, and you are loved. During those times of greatest darkness and deepest longing, we crave the undeniable, perfect love of another. God is holy and is able to give us that kind of unconditional love. It sweeps across our hearts like a wave of intense light and endeavors to bring us ever closer to true life in Jesus Christ. Our faith in God is our foundation. When it is hard to have faith in God (because of blackness), take to heart what Oswald Chambers writes in his classic daily devotional, *My Utmost for His Highest*: "Faith is not a pathetic sentiment, but robust vigorous confidence built on the fact that God is holy love."

Mustard seeds are about one to two millimeters in diameter, which means they are extremely tiny. Matthew 17:20 says that if you have faith as small as a mustard seed, you can move mountains. Mountains are huge obstacles! Nothing will be impossible for you. Therefore, when you are at your lowest place, if you can muster up even the tiniest bit of faith that it will pass, you will be able to do the impossible and make it through. You will go way beyond that point eventually and escape disaster totally.

No matter what our mental/physical concern, we know as children of God we shine like stars in the universe (Phil 2:15). A star's brightness is measured according to how bright it appears from Earth at a standard distance of 32.6 light-years (light-year=distance light travels in one year) (space.com). Imagine how bright that is to be compared to it. With faith and brightness on our side, we have no room for failure in the end. Trust yourself, and above all, trust God. Things will work out.

Questions to Ponder

1. How are you strong?

2. How are you weak? What can you do to strengthen yourself in that area? Think of ways or ask a friend.

3. How do you define faith?

4. What is a mountain that you want moved in your life?

Day 18

STORMS OF LIFE

In the book of Mark (4:35–41), the disciples and Jesus were out on a lake in a boat. A large storm came up and tossed the boat around with much force. The disciples became fearful, but Jesus remained below asleep, unafraid. The disciples wondered why Jesus had no concern for them in such circumstances. Then Jesus told them to have even a tiny amount of faith in him, and he would take care of them. He then quieted the storm.

The storms in our lives are the things that cause anxiety, depression, mood swings, and many other associated disorders. God the Father, Jesus who became flesh, and the Holy Spirit will work miracles in our lives and calm those storms.

Peter stepped out of his boat in the book of Matthew (14:22–33). While his eyes are on Jesus, he sustains his place walking on water toward Jesus. When he takes his eyes off Jesus, he sinks. Our eyes need to always remain fixed on Jesus to stay afloat and walk tall without sinking below the surface of the cares of the world.

Questions to Ponder

1. What is one storm in your life right now?

2. What can you do to keep your eyes fixed on Jesus?

3. What help has God sent your way to quiet the storms in your life?

Day 19

FACING GIANTS

David was the least of Jesse's sons. He was considered smaller and weaker. Despite his inadequacies, he loved and trusted God beyond belief. He had great faith. When the Philistine giant, Goliath, put forth a challenge, only David had the courage to accept that challenge. Not only did David take the challenge, but also, when they recommended armor, he denied its use because it was not needed and was too cumbersome. Only one small stone aimed at just the right spot killed the giant. God's plan was fulfilled.

God has a plan for everyone, and he can use the tiniest thing to fulfill his plan. No matter how inadequate you feel, God can and will use you if you let him. Just like Moses said in the Old Testament in Exodus: "Why are you sending me?" You may say the same thing. He felt so inadequate to free the Israelites from Egypt. God allowed his brother Aaron to help him speak, but then God used Moses to complete his purpose and his plan for Moses's life. When Moses asked God who to tell the people sent him, God said to tell them that "I am" has sent him (Ex 3:14). Since God is "I am," then "You are" a child of God.

Questions to Ponder

1. How do you feel inadequate?

2. What giants are you facing in life right now?

3. How has God been helping you?

Day 20

CARES

"Cast all your anxiety on him because he cares for you" (1 Pt 5:7). God is an always-present help when you need someone or something. The word *cast* brings to mind a fisherman with his fishing pole casting forth his line out as far as he can. It proceeds far away from him at first just as you would be throwing your cares out to God for him to catch. God cares for you so incredibly that he would take your anxieties upon himself and unravel them for you.

A good story to show how God feels about the cares of life and how we deal with them is in Luke 10:38–42. Jesus and his disciples stopped by the home of Martha and Mary in Bethany. Mary had only one thing on her mind, and that was Jesus. She sat right in front of him intently listening to every word he said. Martha, on the other hand, had her mind on other things. She was worried and upset about all the duties of the household that needed to be completed. She even asked Jesus to tell Mary to help her.

Jesus, in a gentle manner, told her that Mary had chosen the better way—full devotion to him. Basically, all of Martha's anxieties and concerns and cares were for naught. We can learn from this.

In life, when we are overcome with the cares of the world, we can remember that only one thing is truly significant. That is glorifying God and learning from him.

Three of the four gospels have another story that shows the importance of letting go to honor God. Jesus's disciples were angered when a woman poured very expensive perfume on Jesus's head. This happened while they were in Bethany in the home of Simon, the leper. The disciples thought the perfume could have been sold and the money given to the poor.

Jesus rebuked them and told them that she had done a beautiful thing. His death would be coming soon, and he said it was in preparation for that. He said that the poor will always be around, but he would not. Of course, he still had compassion for the poor, but it shows the importance of honoring our King and Lord God. He ends by saying that what she has done will be preached around the world; therefore, it must be paramount.

Notice also that the scene was a leper's house. Jesus wasn't afraid to be around all people—even those that others shunned. For instance, another scene in which Jesus welcomes a person of lower standing is in Luke 7:36–50. A sinful woman uses her tears and perfume to wash Jesus's feet with her hair, and she wouldn't even stop kissing his feet.

Jesus told the story of two people owing money—one owing a great amount, the other only a small amount. He said neither could pay back the debt. The man forgave both debts. Jesus asked which one would love him more. Simon answered that it would be the one who had owed more. Therefore, Jesus said this woman loved much and is forgiven. We can learn to pour out our love to God for all our forgiveness.

Questions to Ponder

1. What anxieties do you have?

2. What can you do to lavish God with your love?

3. Who are you able to include in your love? Is there someone who is less fortunate or who is disregarded by others?

4. What has God forgiven you? How much do you love God based on that?

Day 21

ARMOR OF GOD

In the war against mental illness, we need protection against Satan's schemes. He prowls around like a lion waiting to devour his prey. He wants to drag us down by using our insecurities to persuade us that we are not worthy of God's love. The devil can use our mental illness to weaken us and make us vulnerable in the face of battle. Therefore, God wants us to put on an armor—*his* armor.

In Ephesians 6:10–18 the Bible describes the full armor of God. It is our protection in the spiritual battles we face each day. Before describing the armor, Paul says to "stand firm" (Eph 6:14). Durability and resistance are essential for war and battle. One must remain upright and endure the pain and injuries. It involves halting the enemy from destroying your heart. Determine to sustain vigorous steadfastness amidst turmoil, and God will continue to protect you. Even if you are too weak to remain resolute, God will be by your side fighting your battles. God is the general leading the fight. Use the Bible as your battle plan. Follow the manual. Read it daily to remember the guidelines that God has given you. He will guide you.

The belt of truth holds it all together just like a belt holds your pants up. The devil is the father of lies, so we need to hold on tight to what is true and honest. Truth will hold it all together. Just think of what happens when you tell a lie. One lie turns into another lie then another, and then things unravel. People end up hurt and alone.

The breastplate was made of woven chain and used to cover the soldier's vital organs (crosswalk.com). The breastplate of righteousness helps us to remain pure and righteous, thus protecting the heart. The evil one wants us to do impure things. It is up to us to follow God's commands and look to him for guidance to keep our hearts pure. Righteousness will protect our heart.

The good news prepares our feet to be ready. We are to be messengers of the gospel to those who don't know Christ. We can walk with confidence through the fight to reach the lost and win the war. A soldier wants to save his fellow soldiers to bring them home. In our case, that home would be heaven.

Every soldier has a shield. Faith is our shield. Believing and not doubting in something you cannot see or feel will stop the arrows of Satan. His arrows are burning and hot with a fire that can only be extinguished by this shield. We may feel like we are being hit with fire sometimes. You may even literally feel physically hot and feverish when you are in a state of mental incapacity. Know that faith in God can cool you down, and living water will put out those flames of evil and confusion.

Now cover your brain with a helmet—the helmet of salvation. Your thoughts and emotions are covered by the blood of Jesus. He died on the cross to save us from our sins. The brain controls the body, and our whole body is saved through his death, burial, and resurrection.

All that is left is to study and know the word of God. The sword is the Bible. The Holy Spirit is within the word and transforms us when we use this weapon. One of the best ways to combat the devil is to memorize scripture. It provides an arsenal of weaponry to fight the impulses that may arise in your life.

In Ephesians, Paul entreats us to pray. He says to pray "on all occasions with all kinds of prayers and requests." (Eph 6:18). He's very thorough because he uses the word *all* two times. It doesn't matter how weird or trivial a situation may seem at the time, pray. Any occasion deserves prayer. Prayer comes in all shapes and sizes. If you're depressed, anxious, manic, confused, or something of your own making, please know that God is always listening.

Questions to Ponder

1. How do you think truth holds things together?

2. What are some things in your life that you need to remove that are making you impure? Sin in your life?

3. Who do you know who doesn't know Jesus—someone to whom you can share the gospel?

4. What are some things you plan to accomplish to better know the word of God?

5. Write out a prayer expressing whatever thanksgivings or requests you might have about your mental illness or life.

I praise you, for I am fearfully and wonderfully made. Wonderful are your works; my soul knows it very well.

Psalm 139:14

Day 22

DELIVERANCE

Daniel lived a life of devotion to God, and God protected him. When others fell away, he remained true to his calling. He trusted God to bring health and healing to his life. We can learn much from his life. He was persecuted for his faith. When things got tough, he prayed and surrendered himself. We can do the same.

God's sovereignty permeates the book of Daniel. Sovereignty is supreme power or authority. Even though Babylon had conquered Judah, God reigned and showed his mighty muscle. Daniel (Belteshazzar) and his friends, Hananiah (Shadrach), Mishael (Meshach), and Azariah (Abednego), all became immersed in the Babylonian culture without forfeiting their God. Even though we are surrounded by a godless society, we can still stand firm and praise the Lord.

Daniel and his friends went entered training in Babylon. King Nebuchadnezzar wanted to have them ready after three years to serve in his courts. Even though the men were bombarded with Babylonian ideals, they never wavered in their obedience and faith in God.

When a person faces mental illness, many factors come into play. One aspect is food. It doesn't matter how you are sick (physically or mentally); you should eat right. Daniel knew that vegetables and water would keep him healthier than the king's rich food. Daniel told the official to test his decision. Daniel had only vegetables and water for ten days; and, after that, he was healthier than those who ate the king's food. Vegetables and water need to be a large part of our diet to keep our mind and body healthy.

Later in Daniel, the king creates a golden image for the people to worship, but Shadrach, Meshach, and Abednego would not bow down to it. Therefore, the king had them thrown into a blazing furnace. It's interesting to note that they said, "but even if he does not, we want you to know, Your Majesty, that we will not serve your gods or worship the image of gold you have set up" (Dan 3:18). They were talking about the fact that God would save them.

King Nebuchadnezzar was so infuriated that he had "the furnace heated seven times hotter than usual (Dan 3:19). He also had them tied up by some of the strongest men. All of this was to show the power of God. His power is beyond ordinary human power. When the king removed them from the fire, not even a hair on their head was singed, and they didn't even smell like smoke. A fourth figure had even shown up in the furnace to help save them. The king then praised their God, the one true God. Therefore, it all happened for a godly reason—to bring praise to God.

God can bring us through anything in life that seems like a fire. We can be witnesses for him by the way he delivers us. We need to realize that even if he doesn't save us from the fires of life, we still need to follow him.

After a while, the king proclaimed that he was the only one to be worshipped. Daniel was thrown into the lions' den as the decree had said. The lions didn't harm Daniel at all. God was once again praised.

God is truly sovereign, reigning above all nations with a great and mighty power. So, let God save you with his amazing strength. Even if he doesn't bring you out of the fire or away from the lions of this life, continue to serve him above all others.

Never forget to pray. Daniel prayed three times daily on his knees. He is a wonderful example of giving one's life over to God.

Questions to Ponder

1. How has God blessed you and given you power in this world? God had brought Daniel power and prestige in Babylon. Has God put you in charge of anything, like he did Daniel?

2. What worldly things surround you? How do they make it difficult to follow God?

3. What are some situations that have occurred in the past or are currently happening that seem like fires?

4. What are occurrences that could devour you like lions?

5. From what has God delivered you?

6. When have you prayed, but God didn't seem to save you? How did you feel after that?

Day 23

NURTURING A HEALTHY BODY

"Don't you know that you yourselves are God's temple and that God's spirit dwells in your midst?" (1 Cor 3:16). You are, therefore, very special and intricate. As a unique and elaborate building containing such precious treasure, you must endeavor to maintain yourself. Paul calls this temple "sacred" in verse 17, which means it is holy and set apart. Our human bodies require care and nourishment. They need us to cherish them as one would an ancient cathedral.

When we are ill with a disorder of a physical or mental nature, our bodies function abnormally. Therefore, obtaining needed medical aid is of utmost importance. This includes exercise and nutrition. Eating right and exercising are two ways you can begin to strengthen your body. Also, spending quiet times with God can soothe your soul.

It is important to keep appointments with all your needed physicians and therapists. In the case of mental illness, it's good to not only have a psychiatrist but also a therapist. Medicine and therapy can work together.

Nature is also a healing place. Go outside and enjoy the trees, flowers, and animals. Go to a park. Go for a walk. Listen to the birds or the sound of water running in a stream. Swim in a lake or hike a trail to a new location. Open your mind to fresh ideas as to how to free your mind and body from its prison—its prison of discontent. As in a temple, many glorious artifacts are stored inside of you that need to be safeguarded. Put a hedge of protection around them. Monitor your life and find ways to increase the health of the body God has given you.

As God's sacred temple, you have intimate fellowship with God. The temple has God's special presence. The Holy Spirit dwells within you and leads you. You are the maintenance man who is responsible for this temple. Do your job so that your body is healthy and alive.

Questions to Ponder

1. How is your body like a temple? Compare physical traits with a place of worship.

2. What exercise can you do to help your body?

3. How can you improve your eating habits?

4. What do you want to do in nature to clear your mind?

5. When will you have quiet time with God?

Day 24

REACHING CONTENTMENT

In Psalm 37, contentment with little is considered better than wealth. Depression and anxiety can arise when we aren't content with where we are or what we have. Paul learned the secret to contentment. He said, "I can do all things through him who gives me strength" (Phil 4:13). He was talking about Christ Jesus. Also, "godliness with contentment is great gain" (1 Tm 6:6). There is much we can gain through contentment—spiritual peace, physical rest, mental satisfaction, and emotional tranquility. We also receive God's constant presence in times of peril and turmoil.

Peace parallels contentment. In Philippians, the Bible reminds us that peace is beyond our understanding. It "will guard your hearts and your minds in Christ Jesus" (Phil 4:7). Think of a person standing watch at both the door to your heart and your mind. His name is Peace. He keeps out all the many enemies that threaten you. Evil is all around and tries to enter our lives to throw us down.

We are to "seek peace and pursue it" (Ps 34:14). Search it out and grab onto it. It is very important to obtain peace. That flow of emotion will calm the many confusing and rocky feelings caused by some of the mental disorders.

Cognition is a "term that groups together the mental processes of perceiving, recognizing, conceiving, judging, and reasoning" (*Abnormal Psychology*, 8ᵗʰ ed., 49). All of these are crucial in anybody's life to live successfully, but especially in a Christian's life. Christians constantly need to be aware of the world around them. Once these principles come into the brain, we want the right behavior to proceed. In the case of Christians, we turn to Christ and his Word. We want to have the mind of Christ, capturing every thought and putting it under Jesus's rule. If we can change our thoughts, we can, therefore, change our actions.

m the many confusing and rocky feelings caused by some of the mental disorders.

"I should be able to do this or that." "I must do that." "I can't do that." All these statements are falsehoods one tells oneself at one time or another. Our brains are consumed with trillions of ideas and thoughts throughout our lives. From where do these conceptions come? We are each unique; therefore, our thoughts are unique. God created each one of us special and individualized. Our thoughts go along with that. We have free will and our thoughts are our own; yet, as Christians we have boundaries and outcomes to consider.

If you are reading this book, and your mind is completely cluttered, stop! Breathe! Begin to think of a clear blue sky with floating puffy white clouds in it. Each cloud represents a fleeting idea or thought going through your mind. "There are too many," you say. Well, grab an individual one and examine it. Take it one concept at a time. As the Bible says, capture it.

Once you have it in your possession, put it under the "microscope" of your brain and heart. Is it good, pure, right, worthy—all the things that Philippians 4 says to think on? If not, discard that notion. Throw it far away. Dissolve that cloud. Make it disappear forever. Now go to the next cloud, next reflection. Study it! Once again, what does it look like? Is it in obedience to Christ—fulfilling his purpose and bringing joy? Think about the fruit of the Spirit. Would this thought contribute to the growth of the fruit of the Spirit—love, joy, peace, patience, kindness, goodness, and self-control (Gal 5:22–23). If not, push this floating mass far into outer space to be seen no more. Hopefully by now some of the other anxieties and concerns have managed to float on by without notice in the wide expanse of your emotional brain.

Is your mind clearing at all? Keep sweeping it out, but don't forget to talk to God or, at least remain silent to listen to him. Sometimes our brain is too scrambled to pray, so that's when the Holy Spirit bursts on the scene and takes over. He intercedes for us with words that we can't communicate (Rom 8:26). Our emotions may jumble our mental acuity, but God gave us a way out—a light at the end of the tunnel. Sometimes it feels like we are in a tunnel—dark and gloomy. Look ahead, though. God is the light at the end of the tunnel. Plus, the more speculations that can be transformed into bright lights, the brighter the actual tunnel becomes. Negative wonderings disappear so that positive ones can take their place.

The whole concept of capturing thoughts to bring them under Christ's control aids in understanding behavior change. In the secular world, the cognitive behavior therapy stems from the schema that the thoughts we have influence our emotions and behavior. Your emotions and behavior may seem out of control sometimes. Hopefully, you can seize each notion and redesign a new paradigm—one with a better outcome. Grasp the good and look to the future with hope. God will transform you into a new creation.

Questions to Ponder

1. What do you think contentment is?

2. What do you need to be content?

3. How has your mental illness affected your peace?

Day 25

SHOULD, MUST, CAN'T

"I should be able to do this or that." "I must do that." "I can't do that." All these statements are falsehoods you tell yourself at one time or another. Our brains are consumed with trillions of ideas and thoughts throughout our lives. From where do those conceptions come? We are unique; therefore, our thoughts are unique. God created each one of us uniquely and individualized. Our thoughts go along with that. We have free will, and our thoughts are our own. Yet as Christians we have boundaries and outcomes to consider.

"Cognitive restructuring" is a "general term for changing a pattern of thought that is presumed to be causing a disturbed emotion or behavior." (*Abnormal Psychology*, 8th ed.). "In your relationships with one another, have the same mindset as Christ Jesus" (Phil 2:5). Set your minds on things of Christ Jesus, and he will reward you. "For it is God who works in you to will and to act in order to fulfill his good purpose." (Phil 2:13). God has a purpose for your life, and it is wonderful. He is working in you, despite all your shortcomings and mental disorders.

Questions to Ponder

1. What things have you been telling yourself that you should be able to do? Or, that you must do? Or, that you can't do?

2. How can you get the mindset of Christ? What do you need to think?

3. What purpose do you think God has for you?

Day 26

TURNING BAD INTO GOOD

One seventeen-year-old young man in the Bible had a very diverse life. His name was Joseph. Genesis tells us that Israel, or Jacob, loved him "more than any of his other sons." Jacob even gave him a special gift—an ornate robe. Joseph should have been on a high at this point in life, except his brothers hated him.

Joseph tells of dreams he had. In them family members are bowing down to him, represented by sheaves of grain and then the sun, moon, and stars. His brothers hated him even more and were jealous of him.

Joseph's brothers plot to kill him but instead decide to throw him into a pit. Joseph would possibly be in despair at this point. When merchants came by, however, Joseph's brothers decided to sell him to them as a slave. His brothers bloodied Joseph's robe with goat's blood to let their father think that some animal had eaten Joseph.

Genesis 37–45 tells Joseph's story. Joseph finds favor with the Pharaoh and is put in charge of the land. His brothers eventually come to him for aid. When his brothers find out who he is, they are distressed. But Joseph says, "do not be distressed and do not be angry with yourselves for selling me here, because it was to save lives that God sent me ahead of you" (Gn 45:5). God's plans may not seem good at first, but, in the end, they can save lives—like your own. Just obey God and go along with his plans, and he can save your life.

Questions to Ponder

1. What bad things have happened in your life that seem debilitating?

2. How has God put you in a place to help others?

3. What plans do you think God has for you?

Day 27

DEVELOPING WISDOM

"The fear of the Lord is the beginning of wisdom; all who follow his precepts have good understanding" (Ps 111:10). Wisdom can help you deal with mental issues. It gives your insight into what God wants. Fearing God is the start of that wisdom. Fear does not mean being afraid of something but revering God and following his commands. Wisdom begins when we have great awe towards God. Fear of the Lord means we have a profound respect for the Lord, inspired by his greatness, grandeur, and superiority. Sometimes fear causes immobilization. One is so fearful that he or she does not want to move. When we fear the Lord, we should be immobilized from the extreme reverence we feel toward the Lord. We can stop in our tracks to honor God.

Fear can be intense, just like our love for God. We need to channel that energy to please the Lord. Proverbs 19:11 says that "Wisdom yields patience. Wisdom can lead to patience with others and us. We should strive to have wisdom. God will give us wisdom if we ask (James 1:5). "If any of you lacks wisdom, you should ask God, who gives generously to all without finding fault, and it will be given to you" (Jas 1:5).

But what is wisdom? It is making sound decisions based on knowledge and experience. The Bible holds the knowledge we need, and the Holy Spirit helps us experience the presence of God. "All the treasures of wisdom and knowledge" are hidden in Christ Jesus. (Col 2:3). If you search for something hidden, you are excited to find it. We should be enthralled to find and receive wisdom, which includes knowledge.

During our darkest, craziest hours, it is difficult to know what to do. We can get through these times by asking for wisdom and knowledge. God will come through for us. He will never let you falter if we lean on him. Romans says, "Do not be conformed to the pattern of this world but be transformed by the renewing of your mind. Then you will be able to test and approve what God's will is—his good, pleasing, and perfect will" (Rom 12:2). Make your mind new again by following God and not the world. That will allow you to figure out God's will. The Bible says that "the one who is wise saves lives." (Prv 11:30). Let God's wisdom save your life.

Questions to Ponder

1. What do you fear?

2. How is the fear of the Lord different than fear of the unknown?

3. Do you want wisdom? Will you ask God for it?

4. How can you renew your mind? What resources do you have?

5. How can wisdom save your life?

Day 28

RECOGNIZING MIRACLES

Miracles occurred in the Old Testament as well as the New Testament. They are still occurring today. We just need to look for them. Never lose heart about what things can occur. Elisha asked in 1 Kings 4 how he could help a widow who was getting ready to lose her two sons to slavery. He asked what she had, and she said all she had was a small jar of olive oil. He told her to gather up all the empty jars she could find. The oil kept coming to fill all the jars. They sold the oil and paid off their debts.

Elisha went to a house where a boy was lying dead. Elisha prayed to God and then stretched out over the dead boy. He began to have life again. Elisha also healed Naaman after telling him to dip himself in the Jordan seven times. He didn't think that was significant enough to get the job done! Naaman's servants asked him if Elisha had asked something more if he would have done it. Sometimes God asks something basic and simple for us to do, but we think it's not enough. God is a God of simplicity yet complexity. We just need to do exactly what God asks us to do, even if it seems too simple.

In the New Testament the faith of a centurion amazed Jesus.

Matthew 8:5–13 tells the story of a centurion who asks Jesus to heal a paralyzed servant of his. The centurion expressed his great belief because he said Jesus did not even have to come to his house. He believed Jesus could just say the word, and his servant would be healed. God can just say the word, and a miracle can occur.

A miracle is a wonder-filled sign that our spectacular God can do absolutely anything. He may not do something that defies the laws of nature, but he can. Never stop believing that you can have a wonderful life, despite any psychological pain you may have. God can pull you out of the mire and into his great freedom and light. You may feel stuck, like in mud, but God can rescue you.

"Remember the wonders he has done, his miracles, and the judgements he pronounced" (1 Chr 16:12). David appointed people to praise the Lord and declare that God "performs miracles" to display his power (Ps 77:14). His miracles point people in the right direction to repent and be baptized.

Not only did Jesus perform miracles, but Paul did as well. It says, 'God did extraordinary miracles through Paul" (Acts 19:11). "Even handkerchiefs and aprons that had touched him were taken to the sick, and their illnesses were cured, and the evil spirits left them" (Acts 19:12).

Questions to Ponder

1. What kinds of miracles occur today?

2. What do you think about the miracles God performed?

3. What can you do to show your faith in God?

Day 29

CONTEMPLATING DEATH

Paul and Timothy experienced many trials and tribulations in the province of Asia as it says in 2 Corinthians 1:8. Paul says they were "under great pressure, far beyond [their] ability to endure." He says they "despaired of life itself." Does that sound familiar?

In today's world, pressure persists day by day. Many people contemplate suicide. They want a way out. Mental illness may only accentuate that feeling. This does not have to be a "sentence of death" as the Bible calls it. Paul clarifies it by explaining that "this happened that we might not rely on ourselves but on God" (v. 9)

When problems come, release them over to God. Then release them again. Rely on God. Let God carry you through. He will hold onto you and help you endure any troubles. We may not have the ability to endure them, but God does.

"The cords of death entangled me; the anguish of the grave came over me; I was overcome by distress and sorrow. Then I called on the name of the Lord: 'Lord, save me!'" Sometimes we think that we are at the brink of death and even want to die, but "the Lord is gracious and righteous; our God is full of compassion. The Lord protects the unwary; when I was brought low, he saved me" (Ps 116:3–6).

Then you can say to yourself, "Return to your rest, my soul, for the Lord has been good to you" (Ps 116:7). And, in the next verse it says that God will take away your tears and allow you to walk without stumbling. God sees your tears and wants to wipe them dry. With tears in your eyes, it is hard to see your way, and you may falter, but God can clear your pathway.

You may ask yourself, "Why, my soul, are you downcast? Why so disturbed within me?" When you're feeling your lowest, "put your hope in God, for [you] will yet praise him [your] Savior and [your] god" (Ps 42:5).

"As the deer pants for streams of water, so my soul pants for you, my God. My soul thirsts for God, for the living God" (Ps 42:1–2). Therefore, when you are contemplating death, remember that to live we need water and Jesus is the "living water" (Jn 4:10). Drink from his fountain and live. Read his word and bow in prayer to him. He is there.

All of us have a God-given power to overcome whatever obstacles might get in our way. Mental illness does not have to define us or take us over. In Ephesians 3, Paul gives glory to "him who is able to do immeasurably more than all we ask or imagine, according to his power that is at work within us" (v. 20). God's power is truly beyond imagination. We cannot even think or conceive of what God has in store for us. When your brain is foggy or under intense pressure, remember that God is watching out for you with ideas beyond which we can conceive. He knows the way when we don't Trust in him and he will not only bring you back to reality, but he'll take you way beyond all your hopes and dreams. Only God has dreamed up such wonderful things.

Questions to Ponder

1. What trials and tribulations are you experiencing or have experienced?

2. How have you experienced death? Why have you thought about death?

3. How does it make you feel when you cry?

4. What are some of the ways you long for God? How do you feel when you are thirsty?

Day 30

SHARING SALVATION

I couldn't finish this book without telling you the reason for it—Jesus. All of us have sinned and need salvation. Romans tells us that "all have sinned and fall short of the glory of God" (3:23). "The wages of sin is death, but the gift of God is eternal life in Christ Jesus our Lord" (Rom 6:23). In John 3:16 it says that God loved us so much that if we believe in him, we will live eternally. Therefore, it is important to realize you are a sinner. It is also important to believe in Jesus to be saved (Acts 16:30–31). Confess it with your mouth and believe it with your heart (Rom 10:9).

Finally, "repent and be baptized ... for the forgiveness of your sins. And you will receive the gift of the Holy Spirit" (Acts 2:38). What are you to believe? Believe that Jesus came to earth as a man but was the son of God and God himself. He suffered, then died on the cross for our sins. He arose on the third day. Now he is coming again. If we are saved, we will live with him forever in heaven.

Then "live a life worthy of the calling you have received" (Eph 4:1). We receive a calling after Christ saves us. "Be careful, then, how you live not as unwise but as wise, making the most of every opportunity" (Eph 5:15–16). Reach for maturity in Christ. Find out what pleases God and do it.

Meeting with other Christians is important. Church provides many benefits. The Bible says to not give up meeting together in Hebrews 10:25. In Acts 2:42 the early believers "devoted themselves to the apostles' teaching and to fellowship, to the breaking of bread and to prayer."

Tell others your story. "Go and make disciples of all nations, baptizing them in the name of the Father and of the Son and of the Holy Spirit" (Mt 28:19). Jesus took twelve men to be close companions. He made them his disciples to teach them important truths and send them out to spread his word. Using that as an example, each of us can find two or three close friends with which to share the gospel. As a small group we can study together and strengthen each other. Then each person can go out and find his or her own small group. The number of disciples grows exponentially.

One can also witness to one person at a time. If you make just one additional disciple, that disciple can make another. It can have a domino effect. Whatever way you do it, the main thing is to *do* it!

Questions to Ponder

1. Who can you tell about Jesus?

2. What is your story?

3. Who are your close Christian friends with whom you can bond?

Printed in the United States
by Baker & Taylor Publisher Services